101 Ways to See the Light

NEAR-DEATH EXPERIENCES
MADE SIMPLE

By JERRY BIEDERMAN
and LORIN MICHELLE BIEDERMAN

St. Martin's Paperbacks

101 WAYS TO SEE THE LIGHT: NEAR-DEATH EXPERIENCES MADE SIMPLE

Copyright © 1996 by Jerry Biederman and Lorin Michelle Biederman.

All rights reserved. No part of this book may be used or reproduced in any manner whatsoever without written permission except in the case of brief quotations embodied in critical articles or reviews. For information address St. Martin's Press, 175 Fifth Avenue, New York, N.Y. 10010.

ISBN: 0-312-95665-7

Printed in the United States of America

St. Martin's Paperbacks trade paperback edition / January 1996

10 9 8 7 6 5 4 3 2 1

WITH CONTRIBUTIONS BY:

Steven Ackrich
Carole Atkinson
René Dominguez
Jeff Kagan
Andy Shepard
Richard Tanner
Jeryl Uslan

ACKNOWLEDGMENTS

We wish to thank those special people around the world who have shared their near-death experiences and given the rest of us something amazing to wonder about and look forward to.

Thank you, Patti Breitman, the greatest agent on Earth (and in the heavens), who believed in this book and brought it to light.

To our editor, Jennifer Weis, for your sense of humor and for giving us kind words when we needed them. And to

Tina Y. Lee for your hard work and encouragement.

A million and one thanks to our family and friends for laughing with us (and not at us). We appreciate your help, support, love, and always being open to our new ideas. You know who you are, but we wanted everyone else to know:

Steven Ackrich, Carole and Ray Atkinson, Danny Biederman, Esther Biederman, John and Penny Biroc, Debbie and Jay Bolton, Uncle Jules and Aunt Bonnie Bresnick, Mila and Chuck Casper, Kim Gibilterra, Peter Gullerud, Katrina and Robert Harp, Kevin Harris, Uncle Irving, Angela and Ralph Jiminez, Susan Paliscak and Kevin Kinsey, Tina Love, Heather and Mark Needham, Arleta and Gary Owens, Christopher Owens, George Ratner, Tom Reilly, Patti and Craig Rosen, Stan Rosenfeld, Dr. Howard Sawyer, Phil Scheinert, Andrew Shepard, Jason Shulz, Aileen and Steven Sirkin, Henny and Gerry Sills, Jenna Turner, Jeryl and Glen Uslan, Flora and David Wallechinsky, Barbara and Melvin Wolf, and Jackie Wolf.

A special thanks to our nieces and nephews, Illya, Tyler, Carly, Moriah, Allie, and Bond, for being the light of our lives.

INTRODUCTION

Do you tend to avoid death?

Does the thought of passing on make you want to pass out?

Are you afraid of The Great Beyond?

Have no fear. Apparently, death isn't that bad after all. According to the experts, dying can even *improve* your life.

How do they know? Because millions of people around the world have actually died and lived to tell about it! Such a phenomenon is called a "near-death experience." It's a round-trip ticket to Heaven. A dream vacation. The adventure of a lifetime.

These tourists of The Other Side have:

- Journeyed through a wondrous tunnel.
- Been greeted by loving "beings of light."
- Witnessed their own lives in retrospect.
- And felt such a sense of peace and painlessness that they were reluctant to return home.

Sounds great. But the experience doesn't stop there. Once back in their bodies, those who have a brush with death say they are healthier, have a diminished fear of death, and feel a renewed zest for life.

It just makes you want to die, doesn't it?

So, here is *101 WAYS TO SEE THE LIGHT (Near-Death Experiences Made Simple).*

Have a great trip! Just don't forget to leave bread crumbs . . .

9.
Save money on your prescription medicine by using crystals instead.

10.
Get your hand caught in a car door.

11.
Ask a woman who's not pregnant:
"When are you due?"

12.
Get a job painting yellow lines on highways.

15.
Lie down in the aisle of a crowded movie theater and yell, "Fire."

16.
Try to quit smoking.

17.
Say "over my dead body" as often as possible.

18.
Change the diapers of a baby whom you haven't bonded with yet.

19.
Wear a scratch 'n' sniff shirt to the zoo.

20.
Try to treat a cat like a dog.

21.
Trust a teenager with a life-and-death situation.

22.

Become the leader of a Boy Scout troop. During the Parent's Day picnic touch football game, announce that you're gay.

23.
Form a cult in Waco, Texas.

24.
Channel someone who committed suicide.

25.
Pick up a hitchhiker near a prison.

26.
Piss off a postal worker.

29.

Eat a bag of potato chips at a chess tournament.

30.
Kiss your dog while he's eating.

31.
Tell a recovering alcoholic that you spiked his drink.

32.
Get an itch while in deep meditation.

33.
See if what they say about blow dryers
in water is really true.

34.
Tell your dentist you don't need novocaine.

35.
Lick a frozen ice tray.

36.
Watch a friend's vacation video.

37.
When you're having a dream about falling, and you're about to hit the ground, don't wake up.

38.
Go to Mexico and drink the water!

39.
Drive a Japanese car in a Detroit parade.

40.

On your next flight to Europe sit next to an insurance salesman who has just had three cups of coffee.

41.
Invite your mother-in-law to spend the weekend.

42.
Eat anything in the fridge with fur on it.

43.
Become a Big Brother to a Nazi youth.

44.

Pay someone to tie you to a chair in a classroom. Then instruct them to scratch their nails against the blackboard over and over again.

45.
Practice your ESP on one of America's
Most Wanted.

46.
Double dare an IRS agent.

47.
Root for the opposite team at a Raiders game.

48.
Bring a kazoo to a sweat lodge.

49.
Do 101 sit-ups after Thanksgiving dinner.

50.
Put a cup of scalding coffee between
your legs and drive.

51.
Put a "Jehovah's Witnesses Welcome"
sign on your front door.

52.
Go to a mall on the day before Christ-mas.

53.
Wash your wife's favorite white dress
in a load of colors.

54.
Try to put a pink sweater on a pit bull.

55.
Go to a yoga class with a stuffy nose.

56.

Flag golf balls at the driving range in a shirt with the number 250 on the back.

57.

Go to your high school reunion and brag to all of your divorced and broke friends that you're happily married and filthy rich.

58.
Take a big whiff in a high school boys' locker room.

59.
Use toilet paper from Europe.

60.
Shave with a dull razor.

61.
Get caught faking an orgasm by your boyfriend.

62.

Agree to go on a blind date with any-
one your parents choose.

63.
Set up a stand outside the Vatican, and sell condoms and *The Joy of Sex*.

64.
Tell your girlfriend that you've fallen in love with her sister.

65.
Have a heart attack at a medical convention.

66.
Recycle your birth certificate.

67.

Go on an extended vacation around the world disguised as Salman Rushdie.

68.
Quit your job and become a door-to-door asbestos salesman.

69.
Get run over by a kid on a Big Wheel.

70.
Get your period during a full moon.

71.
Tell your husband that you had a "slight accident" in his new car.

72.
Change your flat tire on a hill.

73.
Sneak into the La Brea Tar Pits at night.

74.
Dance on someone's grave.

75.
Pretend a member of the NRA has the hiccups and try to scare him.

76.
Hire a lawyer.

77.
Run for any public office against a Republican millionaire.

78.
Make a voodoo doll of yourself and give it to your dog as a chew toy.

79.

Tie a key to a kite and fly it in a thunderstorm.

80.

Somehow get invited to sing the National Anthem at a baseball game. When singing the song, grab your crotch and spit a lot.

81.
Eat a McRib sandwich.

82.
Go to an open field in Wyoming in the middle of the night and yell, "Take me to your leader!"

83.
While having sex with your wife, scream out your ex-wife's name.

84.
Go into a redneck bar and ask the band to play "YMCA" by the Village People.

87.
Move into your old bedroom at your parents' house.

88.

Visit your grandmother (or borrow someone else's). Say "yes" each and every time Grandma asks if she can fix you a little something to eat.

89.
Wrestle the remote control from Dad.

90.
Become a public school teacher.

91.
Fall asleep on a New York City subway.

92.
Try to merge onto an L.A. freeway.

93.

During a proctology exam, inform the doctor that you don't have insurance.

94.

Show up at a bachelor party dressed as Barney the dinosaur, and tell the guys you're the entertainment.

95.

At your wedding, instead of saying "I do," say, "I'll think about it."

96.

Tell your dad that you really admire and respect him, and that you want to fashion your life after his. Then say, "Not."

99.
Go on a hunger strike until they cure AIDS.

100.
Lose a winning lottery ticket.

101.
Nearly die laughing.

Jerry Biederman

Author Jerry Biederman's most recent book, *Secrets Of A Small Town: The Extraordinary Confessions Of Ordinary People* (Dell, 1993), was the true story of Biederman's journey to a small town "somewhere in America," where he went on a "scavenger hunt" for strangers' secrets. It was a Book-of-the-Month Club selection and was syndicated to over 400 newspapers. *Secrets Of A Small Town* is currently being produced as a Fox television series.

Biederman's first book, *The Do-It-Yourself Bestseller* (Doubleday), included original story contributions by Stephen King, Barbara Taylor Bradford, John Jakes, Ken Follett, Isaac Asimov, Belva Plain, Alvin Toffler, and Irving Wallace (Biederman's uncle). Apart from its popular mass appeal, *The Bestseller* promoted literacy for school children. It was the focus of a major national high school writing competition sponsored by Doubleday.

Another popular Biederman collection, *My First Romance*, was a gathering of autobiographical stories about the first real-life romances of 20 bestselling romance writers. This award-winning book reached the Waldenbooks national bestseller list.

His humorous illustrated book, *He's A Girl!*, was a celebration of "expectant fatherhood." Average fathers at a Los Angeles maternity ward were asked to share their thoughts and feelings on the day of their child's birth.

Biederman's books have been featured on "Good Morning America," and written about in *The New York Times, Los Angeles Times* and *People* magazine.

He lives with his wife, Lorin Michelle, and their dog, Disney.

Lorin Michelle Biederman

Lorin Biederman spent a number of years at Lorimar-Telepictures and Warner Bros. in the International Television Distribution division. She has collaborated on several television shows, including "Box Office America," the international version of "Entertainment Tonight."

Lorin Michelle is also a published poet. She is 31 and lives in Woodland Hills, California.